BOOK 1

THE FIRST AMERICANS PREHISTORY–1600

STUDENT STUDY GUIDE
TO THE REVISED THIRD EDITION

GRADE FIVE

OXFORD
UNIVERSITY PRESS

OXFORD
UNIVERSITY PRESS

Oxford University Press, Inc., publishes works that further
Oxford University's objective of excellence
in research, scholarship, and education.

Oxford New York
Auckland Cape Town Dar es Salaam Hong Kong Karachi
Kuala Lumpur Madrid Melbourne Mexico City Nairobi
New Delhi Shanghai Taipei Toronto

With offices in
Argentina Austria Brazil Chile Czech Republic France Greece
Guatemala Hungary Italy Japan Poland Portugal Singapore
South Korea Switzerland Thailand Turkey Ukraine Vietnam

Published by Oxford University Press, Inc.
198 Madison Avenue, New York, New York, 10016

www.oup.com

Writers: Lynn Brunelle, Sandra Will
Project Editor: Matt Fisher
Project Director: Jacqueline A. Ball
Education Consultant: Diane L. Brooks, Ed.D.
Design: designlabnyc

Casper Grathwohl, Publisher

Library of Congress Cataloging-in-Publication Data is available
ISBN 13: 978-0-19-976730-4

Printed in the United States of America
on acid-free paper

Dear Parents, Guardians, and Students:

This study guide has been created to increase student enjoyment and understanding of *A History of US*.

The study guide offers a wide variety of interactive exercises to support every chapter. At the back of the guide are several copies of a library/media center research log students can use to organize research projects and assignments. Parents or other family members can participate in activities marked "With a Parent or Partner." Adults can help in other ways, too. One important way is to encourage students to create and use a history journal as they work through the exercises in the guide. The journal can simply be an off-the-shelf notebook or three-ring binder used only for this purpose. Some students might like to customize their journals with markers, colored paper, drawings, or computer graphics. No matter what it looks like, a journal is a student's very own place to organize thoughts, practice writing, and make notes on important information. It will serve as a personal report of ongoing progress that a teacher can evaluate regularly. When completed, it will be a source of satisfaction and accomplishment.

Sincerely,

Casper Grathwohl
Publisher

This book belongs to:

_____

CONTENTS

HOW TO USE THE STUDENT STUDY GUIDES TO
A HISTORY OF US

One word describes A History of US: stories. Every book in this series is packed with stories about people who built a brand new country like none before. You will meet presidents and politicians, artists and inventors, ordinary people who did amazing things and had wonderful adventures. The best part is that all the stories are true. All the people are real.

As you read this book, you can enjoy the stories while you build valuable thinking and writing skills. The book will help you meet history-social science content standards and pass important tests. The sample pages below show special features in all the History of US books. Take a look!

Before you read

- Have a notebook or extra paper and a pen handy to make a history journal. A dictionary and thesaurus will help you too.

- Read the chapter title and predict what you will learn from the chapter. Note that often the author often adds humor to her titles with plays on words or **puns**, as in this title.

- Study all maps, photos, and their captions closely. The captions often contain important information you won't find in the text.

A HISTORY OF US

27 *Howe Billy Wished France Wouldn't Join In*

General Howe had already served in America. In 1759 he led Wolfe's troops to seize Quebec.

A **hoop-stay** was part of the stiffening in a skirt; a **jupon** was part of a corset. **Matrons** are married women. The **misses** are single girls; **swains** and **beaux** are young men or boyfriends. **Making love** meant flirting. **British Grenadiers** are part of the royal household's infantry.

Sir William Howe (who was sometimes called Billy Howe) was in charge of all the British forces in America. It was Howe who drove the American army from Long Island to Manhattan. Then he chased it across another river to New Jersey. And, after that, he forced George Washington to flee on—to Pennsylvania. It looked as if it was all over for the rebels. In New Jersey, some 3,000 Americans took an oath of allegiance to the king. But Washington got lucky again. The Europeans didn't like to fight in cold weather.

Sir William settled in New York City for the winter season. Howe thought Washington and his army were done for and could be

Swarming with Beaux

Rebecca Franks was the daughter of a wealthy Philadelphia merchant. Her father was the king's agent in Pennsylvania, and the family were Loyalists. Rebecca visited New York when it was occupied by the British. Her main interest in the war was that it meant New York was full of handsome officers:

My Dear Abby, By the by, few New York ladies know how to entertain company in their own houses unless they introduce the card tables....I don't know a woman or girl that can chat above half an hour, and that on the form of a cap, the colour of a ribbon or the set of a hoop-stay or jupon....Here, you enter a room with a formal set curtsey and after the how do's, 'tis a fine, or a bad day, and those trifling nothings are finish'd, all's a dead calm till the cards are introduced, when you see pleasure dancing in the eyes of all the matrons....The misses, if they have a favorite swain, frequently decline playing for the pleasure of making love....Yesterday the Grenadiers had a race at the Flatlands, and in the afternoon this house swarm'd with beaux and some very smart ones. How the girls wou'd have envy'd me cou'd they have peep'd and seen how I was surrounded.

126

As you read

- Keep a list of questions.
- Note the bold-faced definitions in the margins. They tell you the meanings of important words and terms – ones you may not know.
- Look up other unfamiliar words in a dictionary.

- Note other sidebars or special features. They contain additional information for your enjoyment and to build your understanding. Often sidebars and features contain quotations from primary source documents such as a diary or letter, like this one. Sometimes the primary source item is a cartoon or picture.

finished off in springtime. Besides, Billy Howe loved partying. And some people say he liked the Americans and didn't approve of George III's politics. For reasons that no one is quite sure of, General Howe just took it easy.

But George Washington was no quitter. On Christmas Eve of 1776, in bitter cold, Washington got the Massachusetts fishermen to ferry his men across the Delaware River from Pennsylvania back to New Jersey. The river was clogged with huge chunks of ice. You had to be crazy, or coolly courageous, to go out into that dangerous water. The Hessians, on the other side—at Trenton, New Jersey—were so sure Washington wouldn't cross in such bad weather that they didn't patrol the river. Washington took them by complete surprise.

A week later, Washington left a few men to tend his campfires and fool the enemy. He quietly marched his army to Prince-ton, New Jersey, where he surprised and beat a British force. People in New Jersey forgot the oaths they had sworn to the king. They were Patriots again.

Those weren't big victories that Washington had won, but they certainly helped American morale. And American morale needed help. It still didn't seem as if the colonies had a chance. After all, Great Britain had the most feared army in the world. It was amazing that a group of small colonies would even attempt to fight the powerful British empire. When a large English army (9,500 men and 138 cannons) headed south from Canada in June 1777, many observers thought the rebellion would soon be over.

The army was led by one of Britain's

The Road to Saratoga

ROUTES TAKEN BY BRITISH

ROUTES PLANNED BY BURGOYNE

BATTLE

General Burgoyne's redcoats carried far too much equipment. Each man's boots alone weighed 12 pounds. They took two months to cover 40 miles from Fort Ticonderoga to Saratoga, and lost hundreds of men to American snipers.

127

After you read

- Compare what you have learned with what you thought you would learn before you began the chapter.

The next two pages have models of graphic organizers. You will need these to do the activities for each chapter on the pages after that. Go back to the book as often as you need to. When you've finished each chapter, check off the standards in the box.

GRAPHIC ORGANIZERS

As you read and study history, geography, and the social sciences, you'll start to collect a lot of information. Using a graphic organizer is one way to make information clearer and easier to understand. You can choose from different types of organizers, depending on the information.

OUTLINE

MAIN IDEA: _____

DETAIL: _____

DETAIL: _____

DETAIL: _____

MAIN IDEA: _____

DETAIL: _____

DETAIL: _____

DETAIL: _____

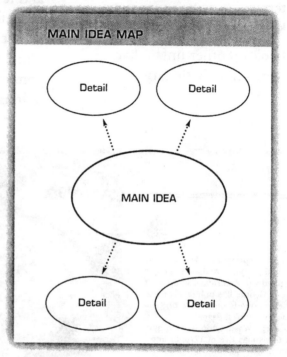

MAIN IDEA MAP

Outline

To build an outline, first identify your main idea. Write this at the top. Then, in the lines below, list the details that support the main idea. Keep adding main ideas and details as you need to.

Main Idea or Concept Map

Write down your main idea or concept in the central circle. Write details in the connecting circles. You can use this form to make a word web, too.

K-W-L CHART

K	W	L
What I Know	What I Want to Know	What I Learned

K-W-L Chart

Before you read a chapter, write down what you already know about a subject in the left column. Skim the chapter. Then write what you want to know in the center column. Then write what you learned in the last column. You can make a two-column version of this. Write what you know in the left column and what you learned after reading the chapter in the right.

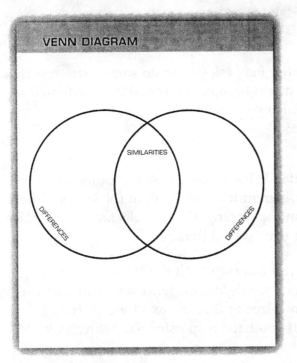

Venn Diagram

These overlapping circles show differences and similarities among topics. Each topic is shown as a circle. Any details the topics have in common go in the areas where those circles overlap. List the differences where the circles do not overlap.

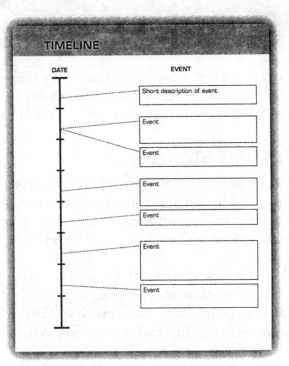

Timeline

A timeline divides a time period into equal chunks of time. Then it shows when events happened during that time. Decide how to divide up the timeline. Then write events in the boxes to the right when they happened. Connect them to the date line.

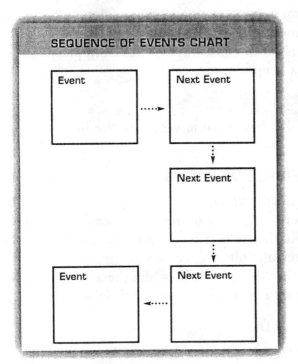

Sequence of Events Chart

Historical events bring about changes. These result in other events and changes. A sequence of events chart uses linked boxes to show how one event leads to another, and then another.

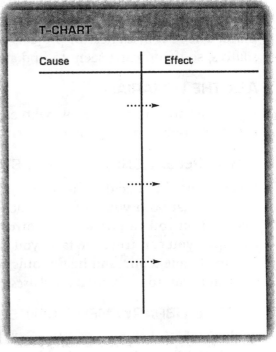

T-Chart

Use this chart to separate information into two columns. To separate causes and effects, list events, or causes, in one column. In the other column, list the change, or effect, each event brought about.

REPORTS AND SPECIAL PROJECTS

Aside from the activities in this Study Guide, your teacher may ask you to do some extra research or reading about American history on your own. Or, you might become interested in a particular story you read in *A History of US* and want to find out more. Do you know where to start?

GETTING STARTED

The back of every History of US book has a section called "More Books to Read." Some of these books are fiction and some are nonfiction. This list is different for each book in the series. When you want to find out more about a particular topic from the reading, these books are a great place to start—and you should be able to find many of them in your school library.

Also, if you're specifically looking for *primary sources*, you can start with the *History of US Sourcebook and Index*. This book is full of *primary sources*, words and evidence about history directly from the people who were involved. This is an excellent place to find the exact words from important speeches and documents. Ask your teacher if you need help using the *Sourcebook*.

DOING RESEARCH

For some of the group projects and assignments in this course, you will need to conduct research either in a library or online. When your teacher asks you to research a topic, remember the following tips:

TO FIND GOOD EVIDENCE, START WITH GOOD SOURCES

Usually, your teacher will expect you to support your research with *primary sources*. Remember that a primary source for an event comes from someone who was there when the event took place. The best evidence for projects and writing assignments always comes from *primary sources*, so if you can't seem to find any right away, keep looking.

ASK THE LIBRARIAN

Librarians are amazing people who can help you find just about anything in the library. If you get stuck, remember to ask a librarian for help.

WHEN RESEARCHING ONLINE, STICK TO CREDIBLE WEBSITES

It can be hard to decide which websites are credible and which are not. To be safe, stick with websites that both you and your teacher trust. There are plenty of online sources that have information you can trust to be correct, and usually they're names you already know. For example, you can trust the facts you get from places like pbs.org, census.gov, historychannel.com, and historyofus.com. In addition to free websites like these, check with your librarian to see which *databases and subscription-based websites* your school can access.

USE THE LIBRARY/MEDIA CENTER RESEARCH LOG

At the back of this study guide, you'll find several copies of a Library/Media Center Research Log. Take one with you to the library or media center, and keep track of your sources. Also, take time to decide how helpful and relevant those sources are.

OTHER RESOURCES

Your school and public library have lots of additional resources to help you with your research. These include videos, DVDs, software, and CDs.

CHAPTER 1 2 3

HISTORY WHY?
AWAY WITH TIME
IN THE BEGINNING

SUMMARY *No matter what their origins, all Americans have something in common: a history based on a belief in democracy. The earliest peoples came in waves over earth bridges between Asia and North America - and might have even come by boat from Asia and Europe.*

ACCESS

To help understand the importance of prehistoric North America, make a "K-W-L" Chart in your history journal like the one on page 8. In the "What I *Know*" column, write what you know about the first humans to come to North America. In the "What I *Want* to Know" column, write three questions you have about the first humans. After you read the chapters, fill out the "What I *Learned*" column with answers to your questions and other information.

WORD BANK   domesticated   Ice Age   glaciers   earth bridge   hunter-gatherers   mammoth

Choose words from the word bank to complete the sentences. One word is not used at all.

1. Ancient people crossed an _____ to get from Asia to America.

2. During the extremely cold period known as the _____, much of Earth was

   covered by rivers of ice called _____.

3. A _____ animal is one that is raised among humans

4. Early humans who came to North America were _____ who followed

   wild animals.

WORD PLAY

In a dictionary, look up the word that was not used. Rewrite the sentence in the chapter in which the word appears using the definition.

_____

_____

CRITICAL THINKING

FACT OR OPINION

A fact is a statement that can be proven. An opinion judges things or people, but cannot be proved or disproved. Put "F" or "O" in front of the sentences below from the chapter.

_____ 1. Nations and people who don't study history sometimes repeat mistakes.

_____ 2. Before we were a nation, we were ruled by England.

_____ 3. Later, when people discover metals and how to use them, there will be an Iron Age and a Bronze Age.

_____ 4. If you look at a map of the world today, you will find the Bering Sea between Asia and Alaska.

_____ 5. That long-gone land between the continents is known as Beringia.

_____ 6. Journeying by sea may have been safer than by land.

_____ 7. Those who came arrived in waves, over centuries, bringing different backgrounds, differerent skills, and different languages.

_____ 8. America was cut off from the rest of the world.

WRITING

Study the timeline on pages 12 and 13. Pick a time period that you would like to return to in a time machine. Write a paragraph describing the first smell, sight, or sound you would experience when you arrived back in that time and place.

SUMMARY *The First Americans spread out in the Americas, adapted to their new surroundings and developed diverse cultures.*

ACCESS

Copy the Main Idea Map from page 8 in your history journal. In the largest circle, write "First Americans." In each of the smaller circles, write one fact that you learn as you read the chapter.

WORD BANK   native   species   extinction   atlatl

Choose words from the word bank to complete the sentences. One word is not used at all.

1. When talking about plants or animals, a word that is has about the same meaning a group is

    _____ .

2. When the climate warmed after the Ice Ages, mammoths faced _____ and eventually died out.

3. A _____ is a person born in a place.

WORD PLAY

In a dictionary, look up the word that was not used. Rewrite the sentence in the chapter in which the word appears, using the definition.

_____

_____

CRITICAL THINKING

MAIN IDEA AND SUPPORTING DETAILS

Each sentence in italics below states a main idea from the chapter. Put a check mark in the blanks in front of all of the sentences that support or tell more about the main idea.

1. *Some people use Native Americans instead of Indians, although the word native is confusing.*

    _____ (a) Anyone who is born in a country is a native of that country, sp ,any of us are native Americans

    _____ (b) Those first Americans were on their own in the New World.

    _____ (c) Native also means to have an origin, or a beginning, in a country.

2. *They invented a dart thrower: a wooden handle with a hooked tip that worked like a missile launcher.*

    _____ (a) It was called an "atlatl."

    _____ (b) When it came to spearheads, theirs were the best.

    _____ (c) The hunter would throw the atlatl as a ballplayers throws a pitch.

3. Others became farmers-among the best in the world.

_____ (a) They took wild plants and bred them, and they developed corn, potatoes, sweet potatoes, and squash.

_____ (b) They grew tobacco, peppers, and tomatoes.

_____ (c) Native American thinkers created mathematically precise calendars.

ALL OVER THE MAP

Study the map "North America 75 Million Years Ago" on page 23. Answer the questions below in your history journal. Use complete sentences.

1. What do you think the climate was like in North America 75 million years ago?

2. How can you tell from the map?

3. Where was your town or state 75 million years ago?

4. Name at least one state that was under water.

WRITING

What "job" would you have preferred in prehistoric times: farmer, hunter, basketweaver, or goldsmith? In your history journal, write a paragraph that explains which type of occupation you would have preferred. Include details about why you would enjoy this type of job. When you are finished, discuss your career choice with a parent, partner, or classmate for extra fun.

CHAPTER 5

PUT ON YOUR EARMUFFS

SUMMARY *The Inuits arrived after Beringia had been covered by water and continue to live in the frosty northern regions to this day.*

ACCESS

The Inuit have an interesting history and culture. As you read the chapter, fill in the outline below with facts you learn about the Inuit's food and clothing.

Inuit Food

DETAIL: _____

DETAIL: _____

DETAIL: _____

Inuit Clothing

DETAIL: _____

DETAIL: _____

DETAIL: _____

WORD BANK   Arctic   subarctic   tundra   taiga   nomad   kayak

Choose words from the word bank to complete the sentences. One word is not used at all.

1. The _____ is the environment closest to the North Pole.

2. The _____ is the region south or below the are closest to the North Pole.

3. A _____ is a person who wanders in search of a food source.

4. A _____ is a frozen, treeless desert.

5. A _____ is a frozen land with forests of pine, spruce, and aspen.

WORD PLAY

Find the word you didn't use on page 28. Notice how it is pronounced. Say it out loud. Then write it in a sentence.

_____

_____

CRITICAL THINKING
SEQUENCE OF EVENTS
Put before or after to complete the sentences below.

1. The Inuit came to North America _____ all other Asian peoples had arrived.

2. The Algonquin named the Inuits "Eskimo" _____ the Inuit had settled in the Arctic.

3. Human people develop art and music _____ they have found food and made clothing.

4. John White and Martin Frobisher came to the arctic _____ the Inuit.

5. Frobisher died _____ he found a waterway between the Atlantic and Pacific oceans.

6. Frobisher was made a knight _____ the battle at Bloody Point.

WRITING
Study the drawing of the battle of Bloody Point on page 27. Imagine that you are an English sailor helping to row one of the boats in the battle. In your history journal, write a diary entry about the battle. Describe your thoughts and feelings, as well as what it was like to be there.

CLIFF DWELLERS AND OTHERS

SUMMARY *In the Four Corners region of the present-day Southwest, stone ruins are reminders of the vanished Anasazi farmers - probably the ancestors of the Pueblo peoples of today.*

ACCESS

As you read about the Anasazi, fill in the main idea map below with facts you learn.

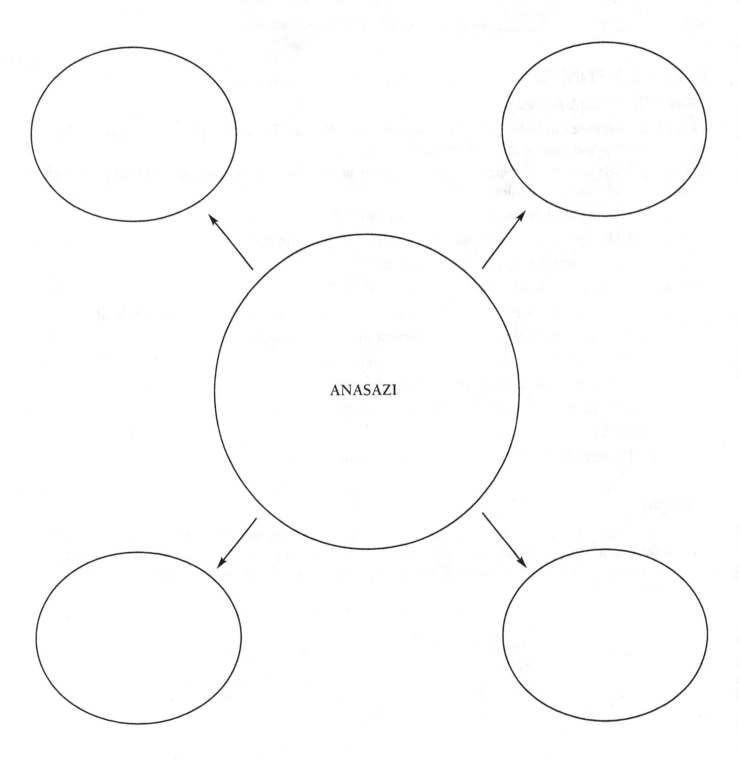

ANASAZI

WORD BANK   Kiva   Pueblo   council   mesa   adobe

Choose words from the word bank to complete the sentences. One word is not used at all.

1. A _____ was a circular structure in which Anasazi men gathered to make laws and other important decisions.

2. A ruling group, or _____, made decisions for the Ansazi.

3. The word for table in Spanish is _____.

4. The _____ was a community of mud-walled buildings.

CRITICAL THINKING

DRAWING CONCLUSIONS

Each of the sentences in italics below is taken from the chapter. Put a check mark in front of all of the conclusions that can be drawn from reading the lines.

1. *You've just left your home, which is part of a 200-room apartment house built on a natural stone shelf on the side of a steep mountain.*

_____ (a) The apartment house was built from stones.

_____ (b) The apartment house had floors built on top of one another.

_____ (c) The apartment house had elevators.

2. *It must have been very hard to build these rooms where they are.*

_____ (a) Building materials had to be brought to the place where the apartment was built.

_____ (b) Builders were not as skilled in ancient times as they are today.

_____ (c) Builders did not have machines in ancient times.

3. *But your cliff home does not keep you safe from drought.*

_____ (a) Anasazi life depended on a steady supply of water.

_____ (b) Cliff homes were dangerous places.

_____ (c) Drought could shrink the supply of food and water.

DESIGN

Study the design patterns on the bowl and pot shown on pages 29 and 30. Draw a circle in your history journal and create your "pottery" design based on the Anasazi style. Use red, brown, and white for colors. When you are finished, share and discuss your design with a parent, partner, or classmate.

CHAPTER 7

THE SHOW-OFFS

SUMMARY *The rich resources of the Pacific Northwest made life easy for its peoples. Their riches also encouraged class-oriented societies in which individual wealth brought prestige.*

ACCESS

The people of the Northwest lived in an area of great resources. To organize the information in this chapter, use the main idea map on page 8. Label the main box "Natural Resources." In the smaller boxes, write one fact that you learn as you read the chapter.

WORD BANK   potlatch   totem   prestige   affluent   commoners

Choose words from the word bank to complete the sentences. One word is not used at all.

1. A large party lasting many days was called a _____.

2. Indians who were wealthy, or _____, threw large parties to show their

_____, or importance, in society.

3. A _____ pole was a carved wooden tower that had symbols of a family's power and rank.

WORD PLAY

Use a thesaurus to find a synonym for the word you did not use. Write a sentence using that word.

_____

_____

CRITICAL THINKING

FACT OR OPINION

A fact is a statement that can be proven. An opinion judges things or people, but cannot be proved or disproved. Put "F" or "O" in front of the sentences below from the chapter.

____ 1. Life is easy for the Indians here in the Northwest, near the great ocean.

____ 2. Using stone tools and fire, Indians of the Northwest Coast cut down gigantic fir trees and hollow out the logs to make their boats.

____ 3. These Native Americans carve animal and human figures on tall fir poles called "totem poles."

____ 4. The Indians of the Northwest Coast like to pile up their goods and show off.

____ 5. There is much feasting at a potlatch.

____ 6. Then the host gives away his finest possessions.

____ 7. Perhaps these Indians are just vain and boastful, like other people in other times and places.

WRITING

Imagine that you are at a potlatch. Look at the drawings in the chapter and describe the scene at the party. What are people eating? What are they wearing? What gifts are being given? What kind of music is being played? What other entertainment is taking place? On the lines below, write an imaginary news article for the "Nootka News," describing the potlatch. For extra fun, include one or two drawings that show the events of the party. When you are finished, discuss your article and pictures with a parent, partner, or classmate.

_____

_____

_____

_____

_____

_____

_____

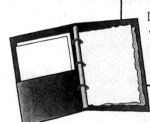

HISTORY JOURNAL

Don't forget to share your history journal with your classmates, and ask if you can see what their journals look like. You might be surprised—and get some new ideas.

CHAPTER 8

TAKING A TOUR

SUMMARY *In the 1400s, geography and climate played big roles in shaping the culture and customs of native peoples. There was no one "typical" Native American culture.*

ACCESS

You may already be familiar with Native American cultures and customs. In your history journal, copy the "K-W-L" chart from page 9. In the first column, write everything you know about Native Americans. Skim the chapter, noticing pictures, captions, headlines, features, and sidebars. In the next column, write everything you wonder about. Go back to this chart after finishing the chapter and write notes in the final column, "What I Learned."

WORD BANK   Tribe   people   sierra

Choose words from the word bank to complete the sentences.

1. A _____ is a range of mountains.

2. A _____ is a community that shares a common ancestry.

3. A _____ is a larger group that speaks the same language.

PICTURE IT

Notice the author's tone and use of vivid imagery to describe the geographic locations and Native American cultures throughout the chapter. Based on her descriptions, draw a picture that illustrates one of the scenes she is describing.

WRITING

Imagine that you are traveling back in time and taking a group of people on a guided tour of North America during the 1400s. In your history journal, write a dialogue that explains the sights, sounds, and smells you will see on your trip. When you are finished, share your dialogue with a parent, partner, or classmate.

PLAINS INDIANS ARE NOT PLAIN AT ALL

SUMMARY *Big game animals disappeared. so hunters on the central plains had to adapt to the harsh prairie environment. They hunted buffalo on foot.*

ACCESS

The Plains Indians have many traditions and strict rules of behavior. In your history journal, copy the main idea map on page 8. In the largest circle, write "Plains Indians." In the smaller circles, write facts that you learn about the Plains Indians as you read the chapter.

WORD BANK   Prairie   teepee

Choose words from the word bank to complete the sentences.

1. A large area of rolling grassy land is called a _____.

2. Plains Indians lived in _____ made of animal skins.

PRIMARY SOURCE

Read the journal excerpt from page 43. Then answer the following questions in your history journal. Use complete sentences.

1. What do the Plains Indians use buffalo skins for?

2. What is a sinew? What is it used for?

3. What other parts of the buffalo do the Plains Indians use? What do they use them for?

WRITING

Pretend that you are a Spaniard accompanying Coronado on his expedition. Write a letter to your family that describes your experiences on your journey.

CHAPTER 10

MOUND FOR MOUND,
THOSE ARE HEAVY HILLS

SUMMARY *The Mound Builders made their mark for over 2,000 years with earthen structures that rivaled Egyptian pyramids.*

10 Mound for
Mound, Those
Are Heavy Hills

ACCESS

Thanks to archaeologists, we know quite a bit about some Mound Builders. In your history journal, copy the "K-W-L" chart from page 8. In the first column, write everything you know about Mound Builders. (If you do not know anything, that is okay.) Skim the chapter, noticing pictures, captions, headlines, features, and sidebars. In the next column, write everything you wonder about. Go back to this chart after finishing the chapter and write notes in the final column, "What I Learned."

WORD BANK   artifact   archaeologist   canine

Choose words from the word bank to complete the sentences.

1. _____ are teeth that are good for tearing food, especially meat.

2. An _____ studies _____.

PRIMARY SOURCE

Study the photo of the great snake of the Serpent Mound on pages 48 and 49. Then answer the following questions in your history journal. Use complete sentences.

1. How large is the mound?

2. Who built the mound?

3. What does it represent?

4. What other types of designs did the Mound Builders incorporate in their work?

WRITING

Pretend that you are an archaeologist in search of uncovering new mounds. In your history journal, write a brief essay that explains how you would go about locating ruins left behind by the great Mound Builders. Where would you look? What type of equipment would you need? If you like, draw diagrams to illustrate your essay. When you are finished, share your work with a parent, partner, or classmate.

SUMMARY *The Eastern Woodland and Iroquois Indians were major enemies. Both groups farmed the land and hunted and gathered food, but their different styles of government kept things tense between the two nations.*

ACCESS

The Iroquois formed a democratic style of government that inspired the Europeans. In your history journal, copy the "K-W-L" chart from page 8. In the first column, write everything you know about the Eastern Woodland and Iroquois Indians. Skim the chapters, noticing pictures, captions, headlines, features, and sidebars. In the next column, write everything you wonder about. Go back to this chart after finishing the chapter and write notes in the final column, "What I learned."

WORD BANK   Slash-and-burn   cultivate   diligently   sachem   unanimous   confederacy   oratory   wampum

Choose words from the word bank to complete the sentences. Two words are not used at all.

1. Indians practiced a kind of farming called _____.

2. The Indians till the soil _____, and because the soil is light, this serves well to _____ it.

3. The chief is called a _____.

4. _____ is valuable and sometimes used as money.

5. Hiawatha was a good speaker and had good _____ skills.

In a dictionary, look up definitions for the two words that you did not use. Use both of these words in complete sentences.

_____

_____

_____

_____

CRITICAL THINKING

COMPARE AND CONTRAST

The phrases below describe the Eastern Woodland and Iroquois Indians. Using the Venn diagram on the following page, sort the phrases above it. Put numbers corresponding to phrases that describe the Eastern Woodland Indians in the circle on the left, and numbers corresponding to phrases that describe the Iroquois in the circle on the right. Put numbers corresponding to phrases that describe both in the center.

1. Formed a democratic confederacy that united five nations

2. Hunter-gatherers who do some farming

3. Farmers who do some hunting and gathering

4. Women are farmers

5. Grandchildren of the great Mound Builders

6. They care about the way that they look

7. Paint themselves in bright colors to celebrate the hunt

8. Live in a one-room house made of narrow tree limbs covered with bark

9. Believe in peace and brotherhood

10. Live in houses that are 150 feet long or longer

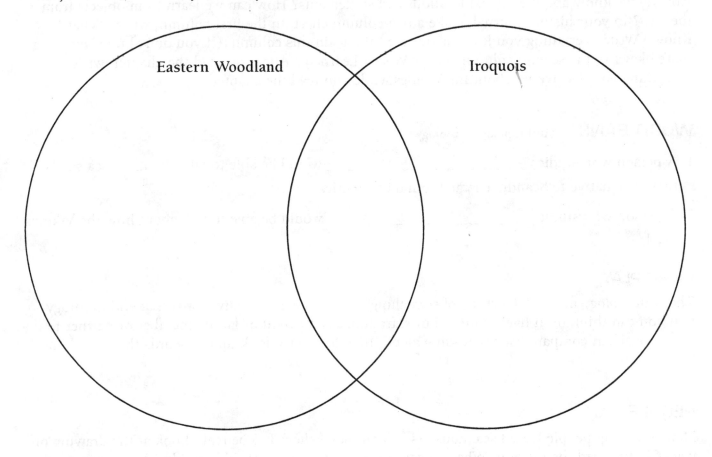

WRITING

Imagine that you are an Eastern Woodland or Iroquois Indian. You can be either an Indian man, woman, or child. In your history journal, write a diary entry that describes a typical day in your life. For even more fun, add illustrations that show the events of your day.

LET'S TURN NORTH

SUMMARY *The Vikings traveled far and dealt with many physical and technological challenges on their journey.*

ACCESS

How do we know about early explorations and settlements? How can we learn from objects from the past? In your history journal, make a two-column chart. In the first column, write "What I Know." Write everything you know about the Vikings in this column. (If you don't know anything, that's okay.) In the second column, write "What I Learned." After you read the chapter, write down everything you discovered about the Vikings while you read the chapter.

WORD BANK   Anthropology   zoology

1. A person who studies _____ would be able to talk about the sea snails that were native to Scandinavia and found in America.

2. A person who studies _____ would be able to talk about how the Vikings lived.

WORD PLAY

The suffix *-ology* means "the study of something." Write down as many words that end in -ology that you can think of in five minutes. For extra fun, ask a parent or family member or partner to do the same. Then compare lists by reading aloud. In a dictionary, look up any words that you do not know.

PEOPLE

Many seagoing people feared sea monsters, which they believed to be real. Look at the drawing on page 62, and read the caption. What do you think sea monsters would look like? In your history journal, create a drawing that shows your interpretation of a sea monster's attack.

WRITING

Look at the photo of the Viking camp remains on page 64. What do you think life was like? What types of things did the Vikings use to make their life easier? Imagine that you are a Viking man, woman, or child. In your history journal, write a diary entry that describes a day in your life at the camp.

CHAPTER 14

THE POWER OF THE PRESS

SUMMARY *During the 15th century, many important inventions, including the printing press, allowed people to learn about other places and sparked people's curiosity to explore new places.*

ACCESS

Can you imagine a time when books were not around? How would you get information or learn new things if there were no books, computers, phones, newspapers, TVs, or radios? In your history journal, copy the two-column chart from page 9. In the left column, list the inventions that were created during the 15th century. In the right column, list the effects of these inventions. When you are finished, share your lists with a partner, family member, or classmate.

WORD BANK   Renaissance scribe compass navigator Indies moveable type

1. A _____ is someone who knows where he is going.

2. A time of rebirth is known as a _____.

3. Navigators use a _____ to help them find their way.

4. _____ is a part of the printing press.

5. Europeans sent sailors to explore the _____.

6. A _____ is a type of profession.

PEOPLE

The following individuals were influential people. In your history journal, write a few sentences about each person that explains what they did and why it was important.

    Henry the Navigator   Marco Polo   Johannes Gutenberg

CRITICAL THINKING

SEQUENCE OF EVENTS

Put the events below in order by writing numbers in the blanks next to each event. (Write "1" next to the earliest event, and so forth.)

_____ Invention of the Printing press   _____ Marco Polo writes a book

_____ Invention of the compass   _____ Viking ships set sail and land in Vinland

_____ Europeans decide to embark upon exploring new lands

WRITING

Imagine that you are a young explorer traveling to a new world. Write a letter to your parents, explaining why you think it is a good idea to go exploring. In your letter, include details about the technological devices that will assist you on your trip.

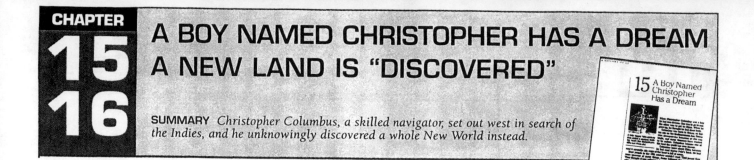

CHAPTER 15 16

A BOY NAMED CHRISTOPHER HAS A DREAM
A NEW LAND IS "DISCOVERED"

SUMMARY *Christopher Columbus, a skilled navigator, set out west in search of the Indies, and he unknowingly discovered a whole New World instead.*

ACCESS

Many explorers, inventors, scientists, and artists have stumbled on wonderful discoveries by accident. In your history journal, copy the sequence of events chart on page 9. As you read the chapters, make a list of all the important events that occurred during Columbus's travels, in the order that they occurred.

WORD BANK

Longitude   latitude   hemispheres   parallels   meridian   mutiny   immunity

Choose words from the word bank to complete the sentences.

1. The Earth is separated into two _____.

2. _____ measures distance in _____ north and south of the equator.

3. _____ measures distance and time east and west of prime _____.

4. If it were not for the vaccinations they had taken, the crew would not have had

_____ against the deadly disease.

5. The crew was plotting a _____ to overthrow the captain.

PEOPLE

What role did each of the following people play in exploration? Match each of these people with their role in exploration of new lands. Record your answers in your history journal.

1. Christopher Columbus

2. Ptolemy

3. King Ferdinand and
   Queen Isabella of Spain

4. Marco Polo

5. Eratosthenes

a. Greek mathematician that made the first accurate calculation
   of the earth's size

b. explorer that discovered the New World.

c. ancient Greek geographer.

d. set out to bring Christianity to the new world.

e. explorer that traveled to China in the 13th century.

MAP

Examine the map on pages 76-77 and answer the following questions on the lines provided. Use complete sentences.

1. What group of islands did Columbus sail through on his voyage?

_____

_____

_____

2. What happened in Hispaniola?

_____

_____

_____

3. How long did it take for land to be sighted?

_____

_____

_____

4. What happened near the Azores?

_____

_____

_____

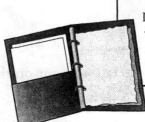

HISTORY JOURNAL

Don't forget to share your history journal with your classmates, and ask if you can see what their journals look like. You might be surprised—and get some new ideas.

THE NEXT VOYAGE
STOWAWAYS: WORMS AND A DOG

SUMMARY *On his second voyage, Columbus still didn't find gold or get to China. But he developed the Columbian Exchange, which brought goods to and from the new and old worlds.*

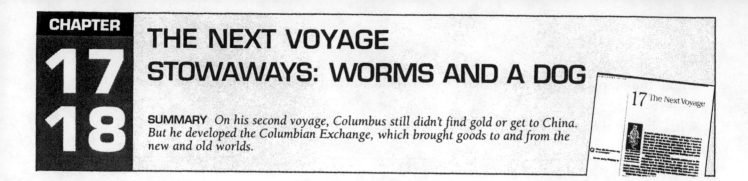

17 The Next Voyage

ACCESS

The outline graphic organizer below can help you organize the information in these chapters. Write down details about each main idea in the lines below.

The Columbian Exchange

DETAIL: _____

DETAIL: _____

DETAIL: _____

Balboa

DETAIL: _____

DETAIL: _____

DETAIL: _____

WORD BANK Columbian Exchange revolution marooned stowaway treason conquistador eclipse

Choose words from the word bank to complete the sentences. One word is not used at all

1. Columbus helped start an agricultural _____.

2. Europeans used the _____ to transfer plants and animals between the new world and the old world.

3. Columbus and his crew were _____ on the island of Jamaica.

4. An _____ of the moon was predicted to occur on the last day of February in 1504.

5. Balboa was a _____, and he was a _____ on a ship heading for Darien.

In a dictionary, look up the word that you did not use. Write that word in a sentence.

_____

_____

CRITICAL THINKING

SEQUENCE OF EVENTS

Put the events below in order by writing numbers in the blanks next to each event. (Write "1" next to the earliest event, and so forth.)

_____ Columbus is marooned on Jamaica.

_____ Balboa discovers the Pacific Ocean.

_____ Columbus and crew begin to starve.

_____ Balboa is a stowaway in a flour barrel on a ship bound for Panama.

_____ Columbus tricks the native people into believing he is in control of the heavens.

_____ Balboa establishes the first permanent European settlement in the Americas.

_____ John Cabot sails across the Atlantic.

ART

Use the space below to draw a cartoon that shows your interpretation of the Columbian Exchange. Make sure that you include pictures of the goods exchanged. Consult page 82 as a reference. When you are finished, share your cartoon with a partner, family member, or classmate. Discuss what your cartoon means.

CHAPTER 19

SAILING AROUND THE WORLD

SUMMARY *Ferdinand Magellan, a Spanish explorer, completed the first European voyage around the world. Now people could start to understand what a big, diverse world it was.*

19 Sailing Around the World

ACCESS

Magellan was an adventurous explorer. In your history journal, create a two-column chart. In the first column, list the traits that you think adventurous people have. In the second column, make a list of Magellan's qualities. Discuss your lists with a partner, family member, or classmate. Consider whether you think Magellan was successful in his quest for adventure.

WORD BANK   strait   Patagones   vastness   putrid

Choose words from the word bank to complete the sentences.

1. He realized the _____ of the ocean.

2. Magellan discovered a _____ near the tip of South America.

3. Magellan and his crew stayed with the _____ for five months.

4. The fruit was _____.

PRIMARY SOURCE

Read the journal entry on page 89. Answer the following questions in your history journal. Use complete sentences.

1. How did Magellan's crew treat the natives that they met during their journey?

2. How does this compare to the way that Columbus treated the natives he encountered?

3. How might you have reacted to the situation? Why?

WRITING

Imagine that you are a sailor accompanying Magellan on his voyage. In your history journal, write a letter to your family explaining your experience on the voyage. For even more fun, include a drawing that illustrates something new you experienced on your trip.

WHAT'S IN A NAME?

SUMMARY *Amerigo Vespucci was the first person to recognize that South America was a continent. A German mapmaker wrote A-M-E-R-I-C-A on a map, and the rest is history.*

ACCESS

Have you ever gone on a trip? What was different about the place that you visited? Did you learn something new? Write about your experience in your history journal.

WORD BANK   antarctic   continent

Choose words from the word bank to complete the sentences.

1. A _____ is a large land mass.

2. The South Pole is also known as the _____.

COMPREHENSION

Christopher Columbus and Amerigo Vespucci had different approaches, and they contributed different things to exploration. Make a two-column chart in your history journal. Label one column "Columbus" and the other column "Vespucci." Write each phrase listed below in the correct column.

Described the South American continent in letters

Continued to search for Cathay

Found the Amazon River

Realized the continent was not China

Brought plants and animals from old world to new world and vice versa

Found pearls and gold

In search of exploration and adventure

In search of riches

COLUMBUS	VESPUCCI

MAP

Look at the map on pages 94-95 and compare this map with the map in your Atlas on pages 178-179. Answer the following questions in your history journal, using complete sentences.

1. List some of the differences between the two maps.

2. Why are the continents shaped differently?

3. How would you describe the style of the map on pages 94-95? Why do you think the mapmaker drew the map in this style?

4. Which map do you think is easier to read? Why?

WRITING

Imagine that you had the opportunity to travel with Amerigo Vespucci or Christopher Columbus. On the lines below, write a brief essay explaining which explorer you would rather accompany on a voyage and why.

_____

_____

_____

_____

_____

_____

_____

_____

_____

_____

_____

ABOUT BELIEFS AND IDEAS

SUMMARY *The Spaniards wanted to convert native peoples the Catholic religion, causing conflict that was often deadly.*

ACCESS

In your history journal, copy the "K-W-L" Chart on page 8. In the first column, write everything you already know about religious tolerance in America. Skim the chapter, noticing pictures, captions, headlines, features, and sidebars. In the next column, write everything you wonder about. Go back to this chart after finishing the chapter and write notes in the final column, "What I Learned."

WORD BANK   religious war   reformer   reformation   culture   convert

Choose words from the word bank to complete the sentences. One word is not used at all.

1. A _____ is someone who wants to change the world and make it better.

2. Some explorers thought that they could serve God by _____ Indians to Christianity.

3. Religious protestors formed their own religions, and the time that they lived in is known as the _____.

4. The Catholics and Protestants were involved in a _____.

In a dictionary, look up the word that you did not use. Write a sentence using that word in your history journal.

CRITICAL THINKING

FACT OR OPINION

A fact is a statement that can be proven. An opinion judges things or people but cannot be proved or disproved. Put F or O in front of the sentences below from the chapter.

_____1. It is always easy to do and think as everyone else does.

_____2. One of the most important reasons to study history: to learn the mistakes of others.

_____3. There was no religious freedom in America at first.

_____4. In 15th-century Europe, most people were Roman Catholic.

_____5. Columbus had many good qualities.

_____6. Martin Luther protested and tried to reform the Catholic church.

_____7. Many people went to the New World to escape from wars of religion.

_____8. Reading history, you will learn about many well-meaning people who did terrible things to others.

WRITING

Imagine that you came to America, seeking religious freedom. On the lines below, write a diary entry that explains why you came to the New World. How do you find your experiences so far? When you are finished, share your writing with a parent, partner, or classmate.

_____

_____

_____

_____

_____

_____

_____

_____

NEW SPAIN

SUMMARY *In 1519, the worlds of the Spaniards and Aztecs collided at the Aztec city of Tenochtitlan. The Aztecs lost.*

ACCESS

The outline graphic organizer on page 8 can help you organize the information in this chapter. Copy this organizer in your history journal. Identify two or more main ideas that related to the Spaniards and the Aztecs. Write these down on the lines labeled "Main Idea." Add details about each main idea in the lines below.

WORD BANK   covet   artisan   immunity   causeway   subdue

Choose words from the word bank to complete the sentences. One word is not used at all.

1. The amazing woodcarvings were created by a local _____.

2. Cortes' men would _____ the gold that they saw.

3. Though the Mayans grew sick and died of the smallpox, the Spaniards had _____ to the disease.

4. The soldiers crashed across the _____ and made their way to the city.

WORD PLAY

The prefix *sub-* means "below" or "under." In three minutes, make a list of as many words that begin with *sub-* that you can think of. For extra fun, have a parent or partner do the same. Then compare lists by reading aloud. In a dictionary, look up any words that you do not know.

PEOPLE

As you read, list two adjectives that describe each of the following people in your history journal. Then explain why you chose them.

    Cortes   Dona Marina   Cuauhtemoc   Moctezuma II

COMPREHENSION

Review the chapter and answer the following questions in your history journal.

1. Who did the Aztecs believe Cortes to be when they saw him?

2. How did the Aztecs get defeated by such a small number of men?

3. How could the Aztecs have done things differently?

WRITING

It is 1519, and you are a citizen of Tenochtitlan. In your history journal, describe the day Cortes arrives in your city. What was your first impression? What happened? Include a drawing that shows your first impression of Cortes.

CHAPTER 23

PONCE DE LEON, PIZARRO, AND SPANISH COLONIES

SUMMARY *After the conquest of the Aztec empire, the Spanish thirsted to find another rich city in the Americas.*

ACCESS

The Spaniards had a goal-to accumulate gold and riches and make Spain a powerful presence in the Americas. Copy the Sequence of Events Chart on page 9 in your history journal. As you read the chapters, write down the events that occurred while Ponce de Leon and Francico Pizarro explored and conquered the Americas.

WORD BANK   fervently   pagan

Choose words from the word bank to complete the sentences.

1. A _____ was anyone who was not a Christian, Muslim, or Jew.

2. Pizarro searched _____ for gold and silver to bring back to Spain.

CRITICAL THINKING

CAUSE AND EFFECT

Match the "causes" in the left column with the "effects" in the right column.

1. Ponce de Leon arrived in Puerto Rico and wanted riches for Spain

a. SO he melted the treasures of the Incan people into bars to send back to Spain.

2. Searching for the Fountain of Youth, Ponce de Leon found a new land filled with flowers

b. SO he conquered Puerto Rico, became governor, and made a fortune.

3. Pizarro believed he should destroy any civilization that wasn't Christian

c. SO he named it Florida.

4. Pizarro wanted the gold and silver for Spain

d. SO he stole their treasures, killed the Incans, and destroyed their city.

PEOPLE

In your history journal, write a few sentences that explains the significance of each of the following people: Ponce de Leon, Atahualpa, Francisco Pizarro.

WRITING

You are a young Incan that has just survived the destruction of your civilization. You want to make sure that your descendents know what your world used to be like before the Spanish destroyed it. Write a letter to your future children, describing life before the arrival of the Spanish. Draw pictures to describe the scenes in your letter. When you are finished, discuss your thoughts with a parent, partner, or classmate.

CHAPTER 24

DOOM, GLOOM, AND A BIT OF CHEER

SUMMARY *The Native American population severely decreased due to disease and war, but their culture survived the conquistadors.*

ACCESS

This chapter is titled "Gloom, Doom, and a Bit of Cheer." What does the gloom and doom represent? What gives a reason to cheer? In your history journal, draw one or two pictures that show your ideas about what the chapter title represents. Share your drawings with a classmate and discuss what they mean.

WORD BANK   mulatto   plague   epidemic   colony   mestizo

Choose words from the word bank to complete the sentences or answer the questions.

1. Which two words describe people with mixed heritage?_____ _____

2. Which two words have to do with disease? _____ _____

3. A _____ is a region controlled by a foreign country.

4. Spaniards married Indians and their children were _____.

5. The Black Death, also know as the _____, was an _____ that began in China and spread west.

WORD PLAY

Following is a list of words that have different words and are considered American/English. Can you trace their origins? In your history journal, create a three-column chart. Label the first column "Spain" and the second column "Africa." The third column should be labeled Native American. Then fill out the chart, placing each word under the country from which it originates.

Adobe	Ranch	Cafeteria	Tornado
Jass	Okra	Voodoo	Yam
Raccoon	Chipmunk	Squash	Toboggan

WRITING

What could have happened if the Native Americans traveled to Europe? Write a newspaper article that describes the arrival of Native Americans in Europe. Be sure to include a headline and any necessary illustrations. When you are finished, compare your article with a classmate's story.

SUMMARY *The Spanish were convinced that the seven cities of gold were located in North America, and they set out to find them.*

ACCESS

In your history journal, copy the sequence of events chart on page 9. Begin with 1528-the year Esteban comes to America as a slave. As you read the chapters, make a list of all the important events that occurred.

WORD BANK   legend   scout   pious   friar

Choose words from the word bank to complete the sentences.

1. A _____ is a member of a Catholic order of holy men.

2. Though he was not as _____ as Fray Marcos, they enlisted Esteban as a _____ to make an expedition to discover the cities.

3. The seven cities of gold was a _____ among the Spanish, and they were desperate to make it real.

PEOPLE

Write a few sentences about each of the following people in your history journal. Be sure to include details about their importance and accomplishments. Use complete sentences.

Esteban   Fray Marcos   Panfilo de Narvaez   Cabeza de Vaca   Coronado   Turk

WRITING

Make a travel poster designed to convince people that the golden city exists. Write a glorified version of the city as if you were writing for a travel company. Be sure to include interesting details and colorful illustrations. When you are finished, share and discuss your poster with a parent, partner, or classmate.

CHAPTER 27

CONQUISTADORS: CALIFORNIA TO FLORIDA

SUMMARY *Spanish conquistadors arrived in Florida and moved west across what is now Texas, New Mexico, and Arizona, looking for gold. The Native Americans in the way were in for more suffering.*

ACCESS

When the conquistadors explored North America, they each had their own agenda and acted accordingly. In your history journal, create a two-column chart. In the first column, list some of the actions the conquistadors performed on their explorations. In the second column, list the effects of the conquistadors' actions. Discuss your lists with a partner, family member, or classmate.

WORD BANK   lance   castastrophe   guerilla   hostage

Choose words from the word bank to complete the sentences.

1. A _____ is a disaster.

2. The Indians used _____ methods to fight the Spaniards.

3. People taken against their will are held _____.

4. The Spaniards used a type of weapon called a _____ to attack the Indians.

TIMELINE

Copy the timeline graphic organizer on page 9 in your history journal. Include the following dates on the dateline: 1492, 1500, 1507, 1510, 1519, 1532, 1536, and 1540. Write what happened during each year in the "Event" boxes on the Timeline.

WRITING

Write a short story in your history journal about an expedition through North America during the 1540s. Your story should remain true to the events surrounding the conquistadors and the time when they explored. However, you may include fictional characters and events in your story. Create drawings to illustrate our story. When you are finished, share your story with a parent, partner, or classmate, or read it to a younger child.

A PLACE CALLED SANTA FE

SUMMARY *The Spanish colony of Santa Fe is founded — the first permanent European colony in the North American West.*

ACCESS

Have you ever tried to win a prize? Gold is a prize that people have attempted to discover for centuries. In your history journal, copy the main idea map from page 8. In the largest circle, write "Quest for Gold." In each of the smaller circles, write a different exploration that was fueled by the search for gold.

WORD BANK   practice   ritual   mission   missionary

Choose words from the word bank to complete the sentences.

1. A _____ is a member of a religious group that tries to convert others to _____ the same religion.

2. Many Indians continued their own _____ in addition to the Catholic ones.

3. Spanish _____ churches, built during the time when Franciscan priests tried to convert Indians to Catholicism are some of the oldest European buildings in North America.

CRITICAL THINKING

SEQUENCE OF EVENTS

The sentences below describe events leading up to the founding of Santa Fe. Put the sentences below in order by writing numbers in the blanks next to each event. (Write "1" next to the earliest event, and so forth.)

_____Many Indians are converted to Catholics.

_____Oñate takes possession of New Mexico.

_____Santa Fe is founded.

_____Oñate begins a Spanish colony in New Mexico.

_____Oñate is stripped of his title and recalled to Mexico by the Spanish.

_____Oñate mistreats the Indians.

_____Word of Oñate's behavior reaches the government of Mexico City.

_____Many Spanish flee.

WRITING

You are a member of the Spanish court. You have just received word of Oñate's experiences in New Mexico. In your history journal, write a letter to the court, describing his behavior. Your letter should include your recommendation as to whether Oñate should be returned to Mexico and why.

LAS CASAS CARES

SUMMARY *A priest named Bartolome de Las Casas protested against harsh Spanish policies and Indian slavery and got a fierce debate going.*

ACCESS

In your history journal, copy the "K-W-L" Chart on page 8. In the first column, write everything you know about the Spaniards' treatment of the Native Americans. Skim the chapter, noticing pictures, captions, headlines, features, and sidebars. In the next column, write everything you wonder about. Go back to this chart after finishing the chapter and write notes in the final column, "What I learned."

WORD BANK   sovereign   superior   subjects   inferior   injustice   unjust

Choose words from the word bank to complete the sentences.

1. The royal rulers or _____ class was thought to be _____ to the people they ruled-their _____.

2. Las Casas was a priest that spoke out against the _____ treatment of the Indians. He didn't think they were _____ and he didn't think they should suffer _____ of giving up their land and their beliefs.

WITH A PARENT OR PARTNER

What do the prefixes *un-* and *in-* mean? Write the definitions in your history journal. Use a dictionary if necessary. Then, in five minutes, write down all the words you can think of that begin with these prefixes. Ask a parent or partner to do the same. Then read your lists to each other. In a dictionary, look up any words either of you doesn't know.

PICTURE IT

After you read the chapter, review the illustrations in the chapter. How do these represent the text? In your history journal, create a drawing the reflects your interpretation of the Spaniards' treatment of the Native Americans as described in the text.

WRITING

Consider Las Casa's point of view about treatment of people and human rights. If he were alive today, what would he think of the current situation in the United States? In your history journal, write a brief essay that explores the equality and human rights from Las Casa's perspective. When you are finished, discuss your writing with a parent, partner, or classmate.

THE BIG PICTURE

SUMMARY *Spain's accumulation of riches and gold made it the most powerful nation in Europe. But Spain's wealth also proved to be its undoing.*

ACCESS

Many events led to the decline of the Spanish empire. In your history journal, copy the Sequence of Events Chart on page 9. As you read the chapter, make a list of all the important events that led up to the Spanish decline.

WORD BANK   freethinker   heretic   economy   inflation

Choose words from the word bank to complete the sentences.

1. _____ can be harmful to any nation's _____.

2. Though dangerous at the time, a person who thought freely about his or her beliefs was a
_____ or a _____.

WITH A PARENT OR PARTNER

A synonym is a word that has the same or nearly the same meaning as another word. Find the pair of synonyms listed above. Then, in five minutes, write down as many pairs of synonyms that you can think of. As a parent or partner to do the same. Then read your lists to each other. In a dictionary, look up any words either of you doesn't know.

CRITICAL THINKING

CAUSE AND EFFECT

Despite all of their gold and riches, Spain's economy weakened. Put a check mark in the blanks next to each reason that explains why Spain began to decline.

_____Industry declined

_____Not enough gold

_____Inflation set in

_____Too much land

_____Taxes went up

_____Peasants left for America

_____Spain fought expensive wars

_____Talented people were forced out because of their beliefs

FROM SPAIN TO ENGLAND TO FRANCE

SUMMARY *Religious conflict was growing in the mid-1500s in Europe. Religious wars between Catholics and Protestants started in Spain, England, and France. People decided to seek religious freedom in America.*

ACCESS

The outline graphic organizer on page 8 can help you organize the information in this chapter. Copy this organizer in your history journal. Identify two or more main ideas that related to the religious conflicts in Europe. Write these down on the lines labeled "Main Idea." Add details about each main idea in the lines below.

WORD BANK   civil war   persecuted

Choose words from the word bank to complete the sentence.

1. The Catholics _____ the Protestants and the Protestants _____
   the Catholics causing a _____ inside many European countries.

WITH A PARENT OR PARTNER

Identify the verb listed above. In five minutes, write down all the words you can think of that have a similar meaning as that verb. Ask a parent or partner to do the same. Then read your lists to each other. In a dictionary, look up any words either of you doesn't know.

CRITICAL THINKING

MAKING INFERENCES

Review the text and answer the following questions in your history journal. Use complete sentences.

1. How did religion create such tension in Europe?

2. How did these religious tensions affect the growing population of America?

3. Who was Bloody Mary?

4. What did she do that earned her the nickname "Bloody Mary?"

WRITING

Imagine that you are living in Spain during the 1500s, and you are not Catholic. What are your choices? In your history journal, write a journal entry that examines the options of what you can do. Be sure to state what you would do and why.

FRANCE IN AMERICA: PIRATES AND ADVENTURERS
RAIN, AMBUSH, AND MURDER

SUMMARY *French explorers, pirates, and seekers of religious freedom arrived in the Americas. England and Spain soon followed. The three countries battled over control of Native American lands.*

ACCESS

The Spanish, English, and French possessed different motivations for coming to the America's. In your history journal, create a three-column chart. Label the first column "Spain" and the second column "England." Then label the third column "France." In each column, make a list of each country's motivations from coming to the New World.

WORD BANK   channel   privateers   pirates   gulf stream

Choose words from the word bank to complete the sentences.

1. Sailed by outlaws and backed by a king _____captured, stole and plundered other ships and split their haul with the royal treasury.

2. _____ stole and kept the loot for themselves.

3. To get the New World treasures back to Europe, ships sailed through the straits of Florida and then through a narrow _____ between the Bahaman Islands and Florida.

4. Because the currents are so strong, the _____ is the best route across the Atlantic.

5. England's _____ sea captain, Francis Drake was bold, brave, and showy. Among other things, he _____ and burned St. Augustine.

PEOPLE

Write a sentence for each of these people, explaining why they are important.

   Ribault   Giovanni de Verrazano   Cartier

MAP

Study the map on page 145. Write answers to the following questions in your history journal. Use complete sentences.

1. Where were the Spanish forts located?

2. Where were the French forts located?

3. Who attached the French and Spanish ships? Why?

4. Where were the Native Americans located?

TIMELINE

Write what happened during each year in the "Event" boxes on the timeline below.

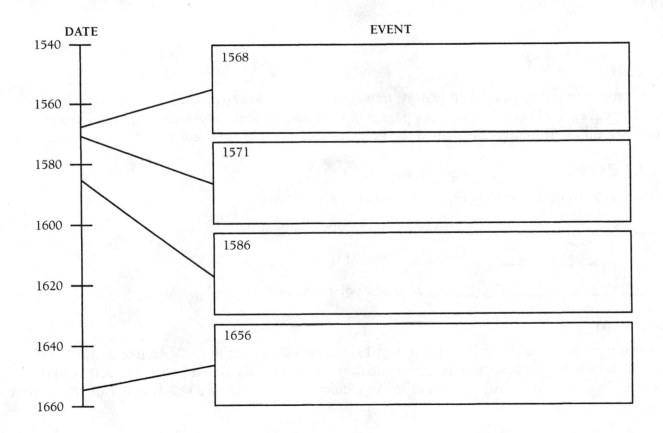

DATE

EVENT

1540

1560

1580

1600

1620

1640

1660

1568

1571

1586

1656

NEW FRANCE

SUMMARY *During the 1600s, the French moved northward to Canada. They traveled down the Mississippi River, and in time a French explorer claimed all the land west of the Mississippi. He named it "Louisiana."*

ACCESS

Do you pay attention to trends? In history, trends can be very powerful and even influence events. Copy the sequence of events chart from page 9 in your history journal. As you read the chapter, write down different trends that shaped the French exploration of the New World.

WORD BANK   Jesuit   portage   robust

Choose words from the word bank to complete the sentences.

1. _____ means strong, healthy, and sturdy.

2. _____ refers to a type of travel.

3. A _____ is a member of a scholarly order of priests.

WORD PLAY

The word portage comes from the French word *porter*, which means to carry. In five minutes, write down all the words you can think of that come from French words. Ask a parent or partner to do the same. Then read your lists to each other. In a dictionary, look up any words either of you doesn't know.

PEOPLE

Write a few sentences for each of these people, explaining why they are important.

 Samuel de Champlain   Jacques Marquette   Louis Joliet   La Salle

WRITING

Read the two quotes on page 147. Imagine you are a young Frenchman attempting to trade with the Indians. What types of things will you trade? How will you obtain them? In your history journal, write a letter home to your family, describing the trading process in America and how it benefits you. Now, imagine that you are an Indian. In your history journal, write a letter to your family, describing the trading process and how it benefits you.

CHAPTER 35

ELIZABETH AND FRIENDS

SUMMARY *Queen Elizabeth inspired a new spirit of patriotism among the English. Under her reign, England emerged as one of the great powers in the world.*

ACCESS

What types of people make a difference? What types of qualities do these people possess? In your history journal, create a two-column chart. Label the first column "Qualities of People That Make a Difference" and the second column "Queen Elizabeth's Qualities." After you read the chapter, complete each column. Then compare your lists. Discuss your lists with a parent, partner, or classmate and explain why you think Queen Elizabeth made such an impact.

WORD BANK

court   Elizabethan Age   chivalry

Choose words from the word bank to complete the sentence. One word is not used at all.

1. The _____ was a great time of creative expression, good taste, good manners,

  and _____.

WORD PLAY

The word "court" has many meanings. Using a dictionary, look up the definitions and use each meaning in a new sentence. Record your sentences in your history journal.

CRITICAL THINKING

DRAWING CONCLUSIONS

During the Elizabethan Age, the arts flourished and people strived for good taste. Put a check mark next to the things that were happening while Elizabeth was queen.

_____Shakespeare writes his plays.

_____Sir Walter Raleigh places his coat over a puddle for Elizabeth to walk over.

_____All people eat with forks.

_____Most people eat with their hands and knives.

_____Cows pull carriages with people inside.

_____Toilets are everywhere.

_____They brushed their teeth with sugar.

_____Only the rich get to eat lots of vegetables.

PICTURE IT

As you read the chapter, pay attention to the author's descriptions of the Elizabethan Age. Then create one or two drawings that illustrate your interpretation of her descriptions. When you are finished, discuss and share your drawings with a parent, partner, or classmate.

UTOPIA IN AMERICA
LOST: A COLONY

SUMMARY *The English came to North America looking for wealth and a new world, but they found disaster at a colony called Roanoke Island.*

ACCESS

The sequence of events chart can help you organize the information in these chapters. Copy the organizer from page 9 into your history journal. As you read the chapter, write down the events that occurred while the English explored and attempted to settle in the New World.

WORD BANK   breakers   proprietor   utopia   Northeaster   royal charter   arrogant

Choose words from the word bank to complete the sentence.

1. The word _____ means the same as landlord.

2. A _____ is a type of storm.

3. Someone who is _____ overestimates their importance.

4. Sir Walter Raleigh took over his brother's _____ and decided to establish a colony in America.

5. In a _____, life is close to being perfect.

6. The _____were very high and made travel quite difficult.

PEOPLE

Write a few sentences about each of these people in your history journal, explaining why each of them was important. Use complete sentences.

   Sir Humphrey Gilbert   Sir Thomas More   Sir Walter Raleigh   John White

WRITING

What does it take to create an ideal community or utopia? In your history journal, write an essay, describing your interpretation of an ideal community. Explain the types of rules you would make, shelters you would build, etc. Include drawings to illustrate your ideas. When you are finished, share and discuss your essay with a parent, partner, or classmate.

CHAPTER

38

AN ARMADA IS A FLEET OF SHIPS

SUMMARY *Sir Francis Drake led the English to victory against the powerful Spanish Armada — setting the stage for their their colonization of North America in the 1600s.*

ACCESS

What is diversity? Everyone who came to America originally came from somewhere else, and most people came to America to be free and experience a better life. In your history journal, write a short paragraph, describing your family's background and how they came to America. When you are finished, share your story with a classmate and learn more about their family's history and diversity.

WORD BANK   isthmus   armada   rampant

Choose words from the word bank to complete the sentence. One word is not used at all.

1. People needed to cross the _____ between North and South America in order to reach the Pacific.

2. Against all odds, the English defeated the Spanish _____.

WITH A PARENT OR PARTNER

In a dictionary, look up the word that you did not use above. Use this word in a sentence. What is a synonym for this word? In five minutes, list as many other synonyms as you can think of that match the word. Ask a parent or partner to do the same. Then read your lists to each other. In a dictionary, look up any words that either of you doesn't know.

PICTURE IT

Using the information from your family history, draw a family tree that shows where you come from and how everyone is related.

WRITING

Imagine that you are a reporter, and you just witness the English defeat of the Spanish Armada. In your history journal, write a newspaper article that explains what you saw.

NAME

LIBRARY / MEDIA CENTER RESEARCH LOG

DUE DATE

What I Need to **Find**

Places I **Know** to Look

Brainstorm: Other Sources and Places to Look

I need to use:

☐ primary
☐ secondary sources.

WHAT I FOUND

Title/Author/Location (call # or URL)

☐ Book/Periodical
☐ Website
☐ Other

☐ Primary Source
☐ Secondary Source

How I Found it

☐ Suggestion
☐ Library Catalog
☐ Browsing
☐ Internet Search
☐ Web link

Rate each source from 1 (low) to 4 (high) in the categories below

helpful

relevant

LIBRARY / MEDIA CENTER RESEARCH LOG

NAME _____

DUE DATE _____

What I Need to **Find**

I need to use:

- ☐ primary
- ☐ secondary

☐ _____ sources.

Places I Know to Look

Brainstorm: Other Sources and Places to Look

WHAT I FOUND

How I Found it

- Suggestion
- Library Catalog
- Browsing
- Internet Search
- Web link

☐ Primary Source
☐ Secondary Source

Rate each source
from 1 (low) to 4 (high)
in the categories below

helpful _____   relevant _____

Title/Author/Location (call # or URL)

- Book/Periodical
- Website
- Other

Printed in the USA
CPSIA information can be obtained
at www.ICGtesting.com
CBHW081038040224
3957CB00009B/19